Thomas Jenkins Semmes

The Civil Law as Transplanted in Louisiana. A Paper Read Before the American Bar Association

Thomas Jenkins Semmes

The Civil Law as Transplanted in Louisiana. A Paper Read Before the American Bar Association

Reprint of the original, first published in 1883.

1st Edition 2024 | ISBN: 978-3-38533-227-0

Verlag (Publisher): Outlook Verlag GmbH, Zeilweg 44, 60439 Frankfurt, Deutschland
Vertretungsberechtigt (Authorized to represent): E. Roepke, Zeilweg 44, 60439 Frankfurt, Deutschland
Druck (Print): Books on Demand GmbH, In de Tarpen 42, 22848 Norderstedt, Deutschland

THE

CIVIL LAW AS TRANSPLANTED IN LOUISIANA.

A PAPER

READ BEFORE THE

AMERICAN BAR ASSOCIATION,

AT

SARATOGA SPRINGS, N. Y.,

August 10th. 1882.

BY

THOMAS J. SEMMES.

[*Reprinted from the Proceedings of the Fifth Annual Meeting of the Association.*]

PHILADELPHIA:
PRESS OF GEORGE S. HARRIS & SONS, 718-721 ARCH STREET.
1883.

THE

CIVIL LAW AS TRANSPLANTED IN LOUISIANA.

A PAPER

READ BEFORE THE

AMERICAN BAR ASSOCIATION.

Compliments of William Beer,

Howard Memorial Library,

New Orleans, La.

THOMAS J. SEMMES.

[*Reprinted from the Proceedings of the Fifth Annual Meeting of the Association.*]

PHILADELPHIA :
PRESS OF GEORGE S. HARRIS & SONS, 718–724 ARCH STREET.
1883.

PAPER

READ BY

THOMAS J. SEMMES.

The Civil Law as Transplanted in Louisiana.

Although the Civil Code of Louisiana is subject to criticism, its excellence, recognized by distinguished jurists, is attested by the fact that no radical change has been made since its adoption in 1825, save the alterations resulting from the abolition of slavery. In other respects the hand of innovation has lightly touched it, the amendments during a period of fifty-seven years being few and unimportant.

Although it deals in definitions and explanations to a considerable extent, and in that respect may be considered, according to Mr. Austin's standard, an improvement on the European codes, yet its principles and distinctions are borrowed from the ancient Roman law, and presuppose a knowledge of it, as modified by the jurisprudence of France and Spain.

This unwritten law constitutes a subsidiary system of jurisprudence, let in by the side of the code, and it governs in the absence of express legislation.

This defect, if defect it be, is not so great as might be imagined; for the Roman law, or at least that portion of it which was made by the writings or opinions of jurisconsults, and which is styled Pandect law, is the most coherent body of law of which we have knowledge. "Although it was made in succession by a series of jurisconsults continuing for more

than two centuries, each of these jurisconsults was so completely possessed of the principles of the Roman law, and
they were all so completely masters of the same mode of rea-
soning from and applying those principles, that their successive works have the coherency commonly belonging only to
the productions of one master mind."

" Leibnitz and others had remarked that of the forty jurisconsults or thereabouts, of excerpts from whose writings the
Pandects are composed, the passages from any one are so
like those from all the others in style and manner, that it is
impossible from internal evidence to distinguish them.
Leibnitz expressed this by rather an odd phrase, borrowed
from the Roman law itself, calling them fungible persons,
res fungibiles being the technical term for articles which are
bought and sold *in genere*, and not individually."

" Each of these writers was master of the Roman law in
its full extent. Each had the whole of its principles con-
stantly present to his mind, and could argue down from them
with the greatest certainty."

It was for this reason Leibnitz said, " that after the writings of the geometricians, there is nothing extant comparable
for force or subtilty with the writings of the Roman jurisconsults; so much nerve is there in them, and so much pro-
fundity." This was due to the influence of stoicism. " In
general, at Rome, a small number of men given up to medi-
tation and enthusiasm preferred Pythagoras and Plato; men
of the world and those who cultivated the natural sciences
were attached to Epicurus; orators and statesmen to the new
Academy; lawyers to the Portico." (Degerando, *Hist. de
Philosoph.*, vol. iii., p. 196.) Cicero compares the Stoics and
Peripatetics, and praises the precision of the former. In his
De Claris Oratoribus, he says:

" *Omnes fere stoici prudentissimi in disserando sint, et id arte
faciant, sintque architecti pene verborum; iidem traducti a dis-*

putando ad dicendum, inopes reperiantur; unum excipio, Cato-
nem.   *   *   *   *   *   *   *
Peripateticorum institutis, commodius fingeretur oratio   *   *
nam ut stoicorum astrictior est oratio, aliquantoque quam aures
populi requirunt; sic illorum, liberior et latior, quam patitur.
consuetudo judicorum et fori."

During the period in which the Louisiana Code has en-
dured almost intact, the spirit of reform in Great Britain
and all the common law states of this Union has revolted
against the pedantry, the fictions, the feudal conceits, and
the artificial theories, with all their train of intricate and
unintelligible modes and distinctions, which learned judges
had vainly attempted to adapt to the wants of modern civil-
ization and has substituted in their place a simplicity sug-
gestive of its classic origin, and bearing the impress of minds
enriched by the study of the Roman law.

My object, however, is not to eulogize the Roman jurisprudence, or to compare it with the common law, whose
principal merit, its advocates think, consists in its being
unwritten; not reflecting that case law, as Mr. Maine says,
is only different from code law because written in a different way.

An attempt to compare the two systems would, I fear,
encounter vigorous outcries from those who fancy the per-
fection of a legal system is to be found in Magna Charta,
extorted from King John by barons and nobles, few of
whom could write their names, and most of whom despised
lawyers and legal science.

This paper has been prepared at the suggestion—I might
almost say at the request—of the committee, who desired that
I should bring to the attention of the Association the existing law of Louisiana, in so far as it differs from the law of
other states of the Union.

I recognize the difficulty of accomplishing the object, for

the field of differentiation is vast, and therefore the sketch must necessarily be meagre and imperfect.

The Louisiana Code consists of a preliminary title and three books:

The first book treats of persons, including corporations.

The second book treats of things, and of the different modifications of ownership.

The third book treats of the different modes of acquiring the ownership of things.

1. The law of persons, in Louisiana, differs but little from that of other states.

The husband of the mother is considered as father of the child conceived during marriage, and the husband cannot, by alleging his natural impotence, disown it, nor can he disown it for cause of adultery, unless its birth has been concealed from him. A child born within six months after marriage may be disowned, but in no case can the father dispute the legitimacy of the child unless he does so within one month after its birth, if he be present; or within two months after his return, if he be absent at the time of birth; or within two months after the discovery of the fraud, if the birth of the child was concealed from him.

If the husband die before the expiration of the time indicated, two months are granted to his heirs to contest the legitimacy of the child, to be counted from the time when the child takes or attempts to take possession of the estate.

The legitimacy of a child born more than three hundred days after the dissolution of the marriage may be questioned; so also when the presumption of paternity is destroyed by the remoteness of the husband from the wife, so as to render cohabitation physically impossible.

This bastardism can only be impressed on the child conceived in wedlock, by judicial proceedings instituted to that end within the period mentioned—his status can be questioned in no other way. But this action *en désaveu de pater-nité* is of very rare occurrence; no such suit is to be found in the Louisiana Reports; but about twenty years ago, the distinguished journalist and publicist, Emile de Girardin, whose first wife was a wit and a beauty, having lived in France separate from his second wife, an English woman, who maintained an establishment in London, produced a sensation in the fashionable circles of Paris by a judgment of disavowal, obtained by him against the child of his second wife, born during the second marriage. The proceedings authorized by the Legitimacy Declaration Act of England, passed in 1858, and by most of the European codes, are similar in principle to the action *en désaveu*. Judgments in such proceedings establish the status of the parties, and are treated as judgments *in rem*, binding on all the world, as was held in Kosciusko's case, 12 Howard, 430.

The code admonishes the wife that she is not at liberty to marry again until ten months after the dissolution of the preceding marriage. This *annus luctus* of the Romans (for the old Roman year was ten months) is designed to prevent a person from being, as Blackstone says, "more than ordinarily legitimate," and according to Coke, invested with the Englishman's glorious common law privilege of selecting either of two fathers.

Children born out of wedlock, of persons capable of contracting marriage, may be legitimated by the subsequent marriage of their father and mother, if the latter acknowledge them in the contract of marriage, or prior thereto, by an act passed in presence of a notary and two witnesses. Incestuous and adulterous bastards cannot be legitimated, nor can they be acknowledged, nor can they inherit. The Code of 1825 prohibited marriage between the white and colored races; the barrier was removed in 1870. A marriage since then, it has been recently held, will legitimate children born while the prohibition was in force. (Suc. of Caldwell, 34, A. 268.)

Fathers and mothers have, during the marriage, the enjoyment or usufruct of the estate of their children until their majority or emancipation.

Emancipation is a judicial act which liberates the minor from the paternal power and of that of tutorship, and confers on him the right to govern himself and administer his property. Emancipation is a Roman expression, but it has lost its primitive significance. Roman emancipation put an end to the paternal power, but so far from terminating that of tutorship, it was the commencement of it, if the emancipated son was a minor under the age of puberty.

A minor of either sex is emancipated by the fact of marriage, but this emancipation is not absolute; it does not confer the power of alienation of immovables.

A qualified emancipation may be granted by the parents to a minor who has attained the age of fifteen years; it is rarely applied for, and is subject to revocation for cause; but at the age of eighteen he can obtain an unlimited emancipation by decree of the court, with the consent of his parents or his tutor.

A marriage contracted in good faith, although declared null, nevertheless produces its civil effects as to the parties and their children; if only one of the parties acted in good faith, the civil effects are to be confined to that party and the children born of the marriage. This is called a putative marriage.

So that where a man married a second time, while his first marriage was undissolved, and the second wife acted in good faith in contracting the marriage, it was decided that the lawful wife and the wife *de facto* were each entitled to one-half of the community property, and that the children of each marriage were entitled as heirs-at-law to succeed to the separate property of their father.

This doctrine enabled Mrs. Gaines to recover the estate of her father, notwithstanding her mother was not divorced from her first husband at the time she married Daniel Clark.

The minor being incapable, a power has been organized by the law to protect him and give him a representative. The power is tutorship, the representative a tutor.

To understand to what sort of power a minor is subjected, we must distinguish three hypotheses:

First. When father and mother are living, the minor is subjected to paternal power without tutorship.

Second. One of the parents being dead, the other surviving, he is subjected to the paternal power and tutorship at the same time.

Third. Both parents being dead, he is subjected to tutorship only. Tutorship is a protective power, as its name indicates. "*Appellantur enim tutores quasi tuitores, atque defensores.*" (*Inst.*, lib. 1, tit. 13, sec. 2.)

In the organization or government of tutorship there are three classes of agents, three orders of authorities: First, the tutor; second, the family meeting; third, the under-tutor. I omit the judicial authority, which, however, has an all important function to perform, that of confirmation.

The tutor is the executive power: he represents the minor. The family meeting is the deliberative body, which votes the funds and holds the purse-strings. The under-tutor is the watchdog or supervisor of the tutor.

The under-tutor cannot act for the minor, except when his interests are opposed to that of the tutor.

The tutor's power is one of administration, and he can do all acts except those of ownership; they require the advice of a family meeting and the approval of the court.

The tutor, therefore, cannot alienate or mortgage the minor's immovables, nor borrow money or purchase an immovable for him, nor expend more than his annual revenues, nor compromise his rights without the advice of a family meeting, homologated by the court.

He must annually invest the surplus funds of the minor in state bonds or mortgages.

The family meeting is composed of five relations designated by the court. They assemble in a notary's office, and after being sworn, deliberate on the affairs of the minor in the presence of the under-tutor. The result of the deliberations is reduced to writing, and submitted to the court for approval.

To protect the minor from the undue influence of his tutor, the code provides that "every agreement which may take place between the tutor and the minor arrived at the age of majority, shall be null and void, unless the same was entered into after the rendering of a full account and delivery of the vouchers, the whole being made to appear, by the receipt of the person to whom the account was rendered, ten days previous to the agreement." (C. C. 361.)

Nor can a minor, until such final settlement, make a gift to his tutor, either by donation *inter vivos*, or testament. (C. C. 479.)

The second book of the code treats of things and the different modifications of ownership.

The idea intended to be conveyed by the term "thing" is better expressed by the French word *bien*, because "thing" comprehends all created objects, and not merely those which can become the property of man.

The word is used in the code to designate those objects which are useful to man, and in which he can acquire a right of property.

Things are corporeal and incorporeal, movable and immovable.

Things are immovable by their nature, such as lands ; or by their destination, or by the object to which they apply.

Things placed on a tract of land by the owner thereof, for its service or improvement, are immovable by destination ; they are movables united to a thing immovable by nature ; hence animals intended for cultivation, implements of husbandry, seed, fodder, and manure are immovables by destination. The *villein regardant*, at the common law, was an immovable by destination. Mills, kettles, vats, and machinery, and such movables as the owner has permanently attached to a building, become immovable by their physical accession to the soil. The attachment is considered permanent if the movables are affixed with mortar or plaster, or cannot be removed without being broken or injured or without injury to the building.

It is thus perceived that movables may be immobilized. This doctrine applies only to such movables as are placed on the land for its service or improvement by *the owner thereof;* it has no application to a tenant who, by virtue of article 2,726, has a " right to remove the improvements and additions which he has made to the thing let, provided he leave it in the state in which he received it. But if these additions be made with lime and cement, the lessor may retain them on paying a fair price." To convert a movable into an immovable, the attachment must be for a permanent purpose, and therefore trees in a nursery, for sale, are not immovables.

It seems to me these regulations, for simplicity and exactness, are preferable to the complicated and uncertain fixture doctrine of the common law.

Things which are immovable from the object to which they apply are incorporeal rights, such as the usufruct of an immovable thing, a servitude established on an immovable estate, or an action for the recovery of such estate. The Roman law applied the terms movable and immovable only to corporeal objects, but the ancient French law extended it to incorporeals.

The French lawyers reasoned that a right in itself was an abstraction ; that its existence could not be conceived unless it was realized by its application to some external object.

Hence they considered it perfectly natural to qualify the right according to the nature of the object. Hence the maxim to be found in Pothier: *"Actio quæ tendit ad mobile mobilis est; actio quæ tendit ad immobile, immobilis est."* (*Pothier de la Commun,* No. 69.)

Indeed, the absolute right of property in an immovable, scientifically considered, is an incorporeal right. It is the type, the standard of all *jura in re;* and the reason why it is not classed as an immovable from the object to which it applies, is that the right absorbs all the utility of the thing; it is confounded with the thing which is the material representative of the right, so that an identification takes place between the right of property and the thing subjected to it ; and hence we say "my house," in order to express the absolute right of property in the house. The right is thus materialized, and becomes a corporeal thing, and is classed as an immovable by nature.

Ownership is defined in our code to be "the right by which a thing belongs to some one in particular, to the exclusion of all other persons." (Art. 488.) This definition is drawn from Pothier. The owner is the master of the thing, the *dominus,* and has absolute dominion over it.

In the *Institutes* of Gaius and Justinian, there is no definition of the right of property or dominion, while Blackstone describes it to be "that sole and despotic dominion which one man claims and exercises over the external things of the world, in total exclusion of the right of any other individual in the universe." (Vol. i., p. 2.) This smacks so strongly of Pothier, that one is tempted to suspect the source whence the polished English commentator drew his inspiration.

The Louisiana Code divides ownership into perfect and imperfect. Ownership is perfect when it is perpetual and unincumbered with any real right towards any third person. It is imperfect when it is to terminate at a certain time, or on a certain condition, or is charged with any real right towards a third person, as a usufruct, use, or servitude.

Perfect ownership gives the right to use, enjoy, and dispose of the thing in the most unlimited manner, provided it is not used in a way prohibited by the laws or ordinances. (Art. 491, C. C.) This description of the rights of perfect ownership corresponds to the definition of ownership given in the French Code. (Art. 544.)

These descriptions are drawn from the civilians, who have improved upon the Roman idea of the *plena potestas* of the owner, which implied the power to use, to enjoy, and to abuse his property. The Latin word *abuti* did not signify a reprehensible use of the property, nor its destruction, but a final and definitive use thereof by alienation: for the Roman law proclaimed as a maxim, " *Expedit rei publicæ re sua ne quis male utatur*. (Just., p. 2, *De his qui sui vel alien.*)

This limitation on the right of property is not recognized in Louisiana, for if the government should become the judge of an abuse of the right of property, it would not be slow to constitute itself the judge of its use, which would be destructive of the true idea of property and of the liberty of its owner.

Ownership carries along with it the right to all the thing produces, and to all that becomes united with it, either naturally or artificially. This is called the right of accession.

The exception to this rule is that of a *bona fide* possessor, who is entitled to the fruits and revenues of property so long as he is ignorant of the defects of his title. He is a *bona fide* possessor who possesses as owner by virtue of a title sufficient in terms to transfer the property, but of the defects of which he is ignorant.

The following estates, or real rights, may be carved out of absolute ownership, usufruct, use, habitation, and servitude:

When an immovable is subject to a usufruct, the owner is said to possess the naked ownership.

Usufruct is the right of enjoyment of a thing, the property of which is vested in another, and to draw from the same all the profits, utility, and advantages which it may produce, without altering the substance of the thing.

That is the definition of a perfect usufruct, and applies to land or other property, which can be enjoyed without change of substance; but an imperfect usufruct may be established on things which would be useless to the usufructuary, if he did not consume them, such as money, grain, liquors.

Imperfect usufruct, therefore, transfers the ownership of things subject to it, but the usufructuary is bound to return to the owner the same quantity, quality, and value, or their estimated price, at the expiration of the usufruct.

Usufruct is an incorporeal thing, because it consists in a right, and may be established by contract, by donation, by testament, or by law; it is an immovable if established on an immovable; a movable if established on that species of property.

It is susceptible of alienation, and if established on an immovable it can be mortgaged; it may be seized for debt, but the usufruct given by law to parents on the estate of their minor child is exempt from seizure.

It expires at the death of the usufructuary, and any words of inheritance contained in the title establishing it are considered not written. It is a real right, but is also a personal servitude, in the sense that its duration is limited by the life of a person, and it is not transmissible; and if that person be a corporation, the usufruct is limited to thirty years, the policy of the law forbidding a perpetual divorce of the usufruct from the naked ownership.

The right of use is also a real right, but a personal servitude; it is a restricted usufruct; it is the right given to any one to make a gratuitous use of a thing belonging to another, or to exact such portion of the fruits it produces as is necessary for his personal wants and those of his family.

The right of habitation is also a real right, but a personal servitude; it is the right of dwelling gratuitously in a house the property of another.

Both of these rights are extinguished in the same manner as the usufruct; they are exclusively personal rights, and cannot be alienated or leased or seized under execution.

Servitudes which affect lands are of two kinds: personal, consisting of usufruct, use, and habitation, which terminate with the life of the beneficiary; real or predial, being those which the owner of an estate enjoys on the neighboring estate, for the benefit of his own estate. They are called predial because they are due from one estate to another and not to the owner personally.

There must be two different estates belonging to two different persons; and if the servitude is established in favor of the person who is owner, and not of his estate, it is personal, and expires with his life.

The predial servitude is purely an accessorial, incorporeal real right, which has no existence separate from the land which it qualifies, and therefore cannot be sold or mortgaged separate from the land to which it adheres; and it remains the same, whatever change may take place in the owners of the two estates; nor is it susceptible of usefruct or of being itself subjected to another servitude.

Its chief characteristic is its passivity. It consists in *patiendo non in faciendo.* The owner of the servient estate is not required to do anything; to abstain or to tolerate are his duties.

Servitutem non ea natura, ut aliquid facias quis, sed ut aliquid patiatur aut non faciat. (Pomponius, l. 15, p. 1, *Dig. de servitut.*)

The principal predial servitudes are the rights of light, of view, of drip, of drain, of support, of passage, of way, of conducting water, of drawing water, of pasture, of burning brick, of taking earth. or sand, etc. An essential condition of their existence is vicinity, so that a direct relation between the two estates can be established.

The code divides servitudes into three classes: 1, Urban and rural; 2, continuous and discontinuous; 3, apparent and non-apparent; but writers add a fourth class, termed by them positive and negative.

1. Urban servitudes are established for the use of houses, whether situated in the city or country, while those for use of lands are termed rural.

2. Apparent servitudes are such as can be seen by exterior works or signs, such as a door, window, or aqueduct. Non-apparent servitudes are such as have no exterior sign of their existence, such as the restriction on the right to build.

3. A continuous servitude is one whose use is or may be continual without the act of man, such as aqueduct, drain, view; a discontinuous or interrupted servitude is such as needs the act of man to be exercised, such as right of way.

4. Rigorously speaking, all servitudes are negative, as they do not require the owner of the servient estate to do anything; but a negative servitude is where neither the owner of the dominant nor of the servient estate is required to do anything, as, for instance, *not* to build; while a positive servitude exists where the owner of the dominant estate is re-

quired to do something, as, for instance, to pass over the land, and imposes on the owner of the servient estate submission to some act.

Whether servitudes could be acquired by prescription was matter of grave discussion among Roman writers. Paulus says: "*Incorporales tamen sunt, et ideo usu non capiuntur;*" in France the maxim prevailed, "*Nulle servitude sans titre.*"

Our code provides that continuous and apparent servitudes may be acquired by possession of ten years, while continuous non-apparent servitudes, and discontinuous or interrupted servitudes, whether apparent or not, can only be acquired by title.

Continuous non-apparent servitudes and discontinuous servitudes cannot be acquired by prescription, because there are no external works or signs which reveal their existence; and not being public or manifest, one of the essential conditions of possession as the foundation of prescription fails, for "such possession must be continuous, uninterrupted, peaceable, public, and unequivocal." (C. C., art. 3487.)

Besides, the law presumes that all acts of interrupted servitudes—such, for instance, as the act of passing over lands—are allowed by tolerance, and are the result of familiarity and good neighborhood, and therefore, being precarious acts, they do not constitute legal possession. This is good policy, for otherwise the right of property would be defiant, egoistic, intractable, and forbid the allowance of good offices.

There is no other *jus in re* or modification of title to property recognized by the law than those I have mentioned; hence the simplicity and intelligibility of titles in Louisiana.

There are no trusts or trustees, no separation of the equitable from the legal title, because there is no distinction between law and equity; there are no contingent remainders, or executory devises, or springing uses; no rule in Shelley's

2

case; no feoffees to uses; no Chudleigh's case, with its *scintilla juris*—a notion as imaginary as the Utopia of Sir Thomas Moore.

The only estates known in Louisiana are the absolute property or fee-simple title; the usufruct, which corresponds in the main to the common law life estate; the rights of use and habitation, and the servitudes; for a lease of immovable property is not an estate in the land, but a personal contract.

A mortgage is not a conveyance of the land, but a mere pledge, the title remaining in the mortgagor, and therefore, in case of his death, a sale of the mortgaged property to pay debts made by order of the probate court, transfers an unincumbered title to the purchaser, the mortgage being shifted from the property to the proceeds of sale.

The fact is, a mortgage right is not a *jus in re;* that is to say, it has no independent existence which effects a dismemberment of the dominion or absolute ownership, like usufruct, use, or servitude, but it is an accessorial real right, which restrains and limits the full and free exercise of the power of the owner. In addition to the mortgage, the code authorizes immovables to be affected by the contract of antichresis, which in some particulars resembles a mortgage.

It differs from a pledge, because that species of contract is confined to movables. It differs from a mortgage, because the antichresis creditor must be put in possession; and in this respect it partakes of the character of pledge, or a Welsh mortgage, but the antichresis merely confers on the creditor the right of reaping the fruits and revenues of the immovable given him in pledge. It does not, like the pledge or mortgage, vest in him a right of preference over other creditors on the *corpus* of the property, and therefore he has no power to cause the property to be seized and sold in default of payment.

Possession also is a real right. What is the foundation of possession, has excited much controversy and metaphysical discussion. Some regard possession as a condition of fact, others a condition of right; certain it is that juridical possession is different from the mere fact of detention or corporeal prehension.

Juridical possession is physical detention or control, accompanied by the *animus* or will to appropriate as owner; the will to appropriate as owner vitalizes physical detention, and converts it into juridical possession.

A man who possesses a thing for another, merely represents another, and his possession is the possession of that other; he has no possession of his own.

Possession, *animo domini*, is recognized by law; it is protected by the right of self-defense, by the right of action, and by the right of juridical assistance to uphold it; it ripens into ownership by the effect of time: and if in good faith, the possessor is entitled to the fruits gathered during his occupancy.

As I have said, there are no other real rights or independent *jura in re* or dismemberments of ownership than those I have mentioned; but the field for the modification of personal relations to property by contract is almost unlimited. It is important to bear this in mind, because the difference between a real and personal right is capital. Real right produces *dominium*; personal only *obligatio*; the former makes the proprietor; the latter, the creditor.

The owner of a real right advances towards the thing, which is its direct object, all powerful and absolute, without the mediation of any debtor; hence he can follow it into whosesoever hands it may be. He is entitled to it in preference to creditors, and it is indivisible as against all persons. Very different is a personal obligation. The creditor cannot follow in the hands of third persons the property alienated by the debtor.   He has no greater right than other creditors, prior or posterior to him, since all hold by the same title, *ex persona debitoris;* and his right is divided on the debtor's decease into as many fractions as there are heirs; for the person of the debtor is then juridically divided into as many persons as there are heirs.

I now turn to the different modes of acquiring ownership, treated of in the third book of the code.

The code enumerates three modes of acquisition:

1. Succession, legal or testamentary.
2. By the effect of obligations.
3. By the operation of law.

In the Roman law a contract did not effect a change of title to property, the object of the contract.   This change of title was only produced by some fact posterior to the contract, such as delivery.   In Louisiana the translation of title to a determinate thing is the direct and immediate effect of the contract.

When the object of the contract is not a determinate thing, but only one of a species, it is delivery which effects the transfer of ownership.

Things are acquired by gratuitous or onerous title.   When I give a value in exchange for what I acquire, it is an acquisition by onerous title.   Donation is a mode of acquiring by gratuitous title.

There are many differences between these two modes of acquisition.   A sale is formed by mere consent of the parties proved in any mode.   Donation is a solemn contract which can only be proved by an authentic act; that is to say, by an act passed in the presence of a notary and two witnesses. Such an act is closely assimilated to a judicial record, and constitutes full proof against the parties.   Any other form of donation *inter vivos* is null, except the manual gift of corporeal movables accompanied by delivery.

In onerous contracts, any condition contrary to law and good morals vitiate them ; while in donations, such conditions are reputed not written; the donations stand, but the conditions are null.

There is a greater capacity to dispose or acquire by onerous, than by gratuitous title. For instance, none of the limitations contained in articles 1,481, 1,483, 1,486, 1,488, 1,489 and 1,490 apply to sales between the same parties. Article 1,481 prohibits a gift to a concubine exceeding one-tenth of the estate of the donor.

Article 1,483 prohibits gifts to natural children by their father beyond what is necessary for maintenance, whenever the donor leaves legitimate descendants.

Article 1,486 prohibits gifts to natural children by their father in excess of one-fourth of the estate of the donor, if he leave legitimate ascendants, or brothers, or sisters, or descendants from them; or in excess of one-third, if he leave more remote collateral relations. In all cases in which the father gives to natural children the portion permitted him by the law to dispose of, he is obliged to give the rest of his property to his legitimate relations, or to some public institution; every other disposition is null. (Art. 1,487, C. C.) It is manifest that the policy of such enactments is in the interest of morality and of society. Immorality, which darkens the soul, impairs the freedom of gratuitous disposition.

Article 1,489 prohibits donations to the professionally attending surgeons, physicians, or ministers of the gospel, if made during the last illness of the donor.

Article 1,490 avoids a donation made to a stranger, when the laws of his country prohibit a similar donation, in favor of a citizen of Louisiana.

On the other hand, sales between husband and wife are prohibited, while donations are allowed.

Things are also acquired by universal title or particular title.

I acquire a universality when a person transmits to me not *such* an object rather than another, but the whole or the universality of his property, or an aliquot part of the whole, such as a third or a fourth of all his property.

I acquire by particular title when a person gives to me one or many determinate things, considered individually or isolatedly.

The interest in this distinction consists principally in the obligation imposed on those who acquire by universal title to pay the debts of their author ; while no such obligation is attached to an acquisition by particular title.

The *universitas juris* occurs when one man is invested with the legal clothing of another, becoming, not at successive periods, but at the same moment, *uno ictu*, subject to all his liabilities, and entitled to all his rights.

To constitute universal succession, the transmission of the aggregate of rights and duties must take place at the same moment and in virtue of the same legal capacity in the recipient.

The succession of an assignee in bankruptcy to all the property of the bankrupt is a universal succession, although he is liable for debts only to the extent of the assets.

In consequence of the difference between realty and personalty at common law, there is no universal succession, though there is a succession under universal title, as the title to all the personalty vests in the executor or administrator, and all the realty in the heir. Besides universal legatees or instituted heirs, there are legatees under universal title, where a testator bequeaths a half or a third of all his immovables or all his movables, or a fixed proportion of all his immovables or of all his movables. (C. C. art. 1,612.) Such legatee by universal title is bound for his proportion of debts.

Inheritance is a universal succession occuring at death. The heir, or group of heirs, if there be more than one, represents the dead man and at the moment of his death; is clothed with his entire legal person, and steps into all his rights and duties. Such inheritance is expressed by the French axiom, " *Le mort saisit le vif.*"

It is one of the most important principles of the civil law that the debts are a charge on the universality of goods, on the entire patrimony, and not on any specific object separately considered—"*Æs alienum est onus universi patrimonii, non certarum rerum.*"

Intestate succession is in general a mode of acquisition by universal title; the exception to the transmission of the universality to the intestate's heirs, is the successoral return provided for in articles 908 and 909.

These articles also constitute the only exception to the rule mentioned in article 885, which declares "that the law does not take into consideration the origin or the nature of the property in order to regulate the succession."

Articles 908 and 909 provide "that ascendants, to the exclusion of all others, inherit the immovables given by them to their children or their descendants of a more remote degree, who die without posterity, when these objects are found in the succession."

"Ascendants have also the right to take from the succession of their child or descendant, who dies without issue, the dowry they may have settled in money upon her."

Succession is the transmission of the universality of rights and obligations of the deceased to his heirs. (" *Hæreditas nihil aliud est quam successio in universum jus quod defunctus habuit.*")

There are three sorts—testamentary, legal, and irregular. The legal succession is founded on legitimate blood relationship; the irregular is that established by law in favor of certain persons, or of the state, in default of relations.

Natural children, duly acknowledged, but not adulterous or incestuous bastards, are irregular heirs. They inherit from their mother, to the exclusion of all relations except lawful children. They inherit from their father, to the exclusion of the state only.

In what are called the customary provinces of France, in ancient times, there was no such thing as testamentary heir. In those provinces it was said: " *Hæredes gignuntur, non scribuntur,*" or " *Deus hæredem facere potest, non homo.*"

The Louisiana Code admits the institution of an heir by testament, as was the fashion—I might almost say the passion —in ancient Rome; for a singular horror of dying intestate characterized the Roman.

This vehement distaste for an intestacy, to which Roman society remained constant for so many ages, has been attributed to the unnatural distribution of property by the ancient *jus civile,* which recognized only three orders of successors— unemancipated children, the nearest grade of the agnate kindred, and the gentiles.

Emancipated sons were excluded by the nearest grade of the agnate kindred, and no part of the inheritance was given to any relative united to the deceased through female descents.

All other branches of the family were excluded, and the inheritance went to the gentiles, or entire body of Roman citizens bearing the same name as the deceased.

In the ascertainment of heirship, the civil law method of computing degrees of consanguinity is adopted.

In case of brothers and sisters of the whole and half blood inheriting from one another, the succession is first divided equally between the paternal and maternal lines. German brothers and sisters take part in both lines; the paternal and maternal brothers and sisters each in their respective lines only.

A succession is acquired by the heir, legal or testamentary, immediately on the death of the deceased. He is seized from that moment of the entire estate, real and personal.

By the Roman law, and under the Code of 1808, which was the first attempt at codification in Louisiana, until the acceptance or renunciation of the heir, the succession was considered a fictitious being, *hæreditus jacens,* representing in every respect the deceased.

But the Code of 1825 considers the heir as having succeeded to the deceased from the instant of his death. Yet the right of the heir is in suspense until he accepts or rejects the succession; if he accepts, he is considered as having succeeded to the deceased at the moment of his death; if he renounces, he is considered as never having acquired the succession, and the next heir succeeds, as if he were originally the nearest heir.

But some heirs are unworthy; as, for instance, those convicted of having killed or attempted to kill the deceased.

The unworthy heir remains seized of the succession until deprived of it by a judgment declaring him unworthy.

Children are forced heirs, so that donations *inter vivos* or *mortis causa* cannot exceed two-thirds of the disposer's property, if he leaves one child, one-half if he leaves two children, or one-third if he leaves three or any greater number.

Father and mother, if their be no children, are forced heirs to the extent of one-third. On the death of the donor, if the donations made during his life exceed the disposable portion, the forced heir can, by suit for reduction of donations, compel the donees to make good his legitime.

So that if a man gives away in his lifetime $100,000, and dies insolvent, his child may recover one-third of the amount from the donees. This right is personal to the heir, and cannot be exercised by creditors of the donor; nor can it be exercised until the death of the donor, for it is a right to that portion of the donor's estate reserved by law to his heir.

Forced heirs are so called because the donor cannot deprive them of their portion of the estate reserved to them by law, which is called the legitime.

They may be deprived of the legitime by disinherison for one of the causes enumerated in Arts. 1,621 and 1,623 of the code, which must be expressed in the will, and its existence proved. Among such causes is mentioned the marriage of a minor without consent of parents.

If the heir chooses to accept the succession unconditionally, there is no inventory, no administration, no expense; he is put in possession at once, and represents the person of the deceased, and as such is liable for all his obligations, whether the property inherited be sufficient or not to pay them.

If the heir is a minor, or, being a major, prefers an administration, he accepts with benefit of inventory. In such case he is not put into possession until the estate is wound up by an administrator, who takes an inventory and gives bond, and then the heir receives any surplus remaining as the result of the liquidation. Acceptance with benefit of inventory means that the obligations of the heir are to be limited to the value of the estate inherited by him. Hence an inventory is made of the effects of the succession, and they are sold under order of court, and the heir incurs no responsibility to creditors beyond the amount coming into his hands. An unconditional acceptance renders the heir absolutely liable for all the debts of the deceased, whether the property inherited be sufficient for that purpose or not; there is no inventory in that case, and no administration; hence a minor cannot accept a succession unconditionally.

The system of administration, whether by an executor or administrator, is similar to that in other states, except that the title or legal seizin of all the property, real and personal, is vested in the heir, the administrator having possession, however, for the purpose of administration, and the probate court orders its sale to pay debts and legacies.

If there are two or more heirs, they inherit equal shares, and become liable each for his virile share of the obligations of the deceased. In other words, all the obligations of the deceased, except such as are indivisible, are split into as many fractions as there are heirs, who become, in fact, separate debtors.

The consequences of this splitting are, 1st, each heir is only bound for his virile share; 2d, if one heir becomes insolvent, it is the loss of the creditor. This supposes that the heirs have accepted unconditionally—that is to say, without benefit of inventory; for if the estate is under administration in the hands of an executor or administrator, the insolvency of one heir does not affect the creditor of the deceased; and even if the heirs should accept the succession unconditionally, the creditor, by demanding a separation of patrimony—that is to say, a separation of the property of the deceased from that of the heirs—can by that means prevent the creditors of the heir from being paid out of the assets of the deceased, to the prejudice of the creditors of the deceased. Such separation of patrimony can also be demanded by the creditors of the heirs.

But if the object of the obligation be not susceptible of a divided execution, then it is said to be indivisible, and each heir is liable for the whole.

In point of practice, this splitting of obligations does not occur except in cases where the heirs are all majors, and accept the succession unconditionally, and take possession of its effects without benefit of inventory. In all other cases there is a judicial administration, and the administrator or executor, as to creditors, represents the entire succession, and the property, real or personal, in his possession, is sold, under decree of court, to pay debts and legacies.

But an executor is regarded as the mandatary of the testator. It is a peculiar sort of agency, as it commences at the period when all other agencies terminate.

If the succession be testamentary, and the instituted or testamentary heirs receive different shares of the universality of the succession—say one is heir for half, one for a quarter, and two others for one-eighth each—the obligations of the deceased are split in the same proportions, and the heirs are liable for debts in those proportions.

A legatee, unless he be a legatee under universal title, is not responsible for debts; he cannot obtain his legacy until the debts are paid. The difference between a testamentary heir and a legatee is that the latter does not participate in the universality of the succession. He takes by particular title, and therefore does not represent the *universum jus* of the deceased.

Entailments, called by the civilians "substitutions," as well as trusts or *fidei commissa*, are prohibited. "Every disposition by which the donee, the heir, or the legatee is charged to preserve or to return a thing to a third person, is null even with regard to the donee, the instituted heir, or the legatee." (C. C. 1,520.)

The term "substitution" is derived from *sub institutio*, or secondary institution of heir; as, for instance, I give to A, and if he die without heirs, the estate is to go to B.

To constitute a substitution, three things are required :

1. An obligation to preserve the thing.
2. To preserve it until the death of the donee.
3. To deliver it at the death of the donee to another person.

Such a disposition, it is perceived, ties up the property, prevents its alienation, and designates who shall succeed as heir on the death of the donee.

The prohibition of the code embraces, with the substitutions and *fidei commissa* of the Roman, Spanish, and French laws, the trust estates of the English chancery system. The prohibition was made in the interest of public order, to preserve the simplicity of titles, which were all allodial.

The distinction between a substitution, and the donation of the usufruct to one person and the naked property to another is that, in the latter case, the naked property vests immediately, and there must, therefore, be some person *in esse* at the time the donation goes into effect, having capacity at that time to receive it; whereas the person who is to take under a substitution may be unknown to the donor, or may not be in existence at the time of the execution of the donation.

Wills are treated of in the code under the title, of donations *mortis causa*.

The olographic will requires no witnesses. It must be entirely written, dated, and signed by the hand of the testator.

The olographic will is of Roman origin. It was authorized by the Emperors Theodosius and Valentinian, but subsequently Justinian, in the 107th Novel, required witnesses, unless the will was executed by an ascendant for the sole purpose of making a partition of his entire estate among his descendants. By an ordinance of Louis XIII., in 1620, olographic wills were permitted; but in the *droit écrit* provinces, the parliaments, having refused to register the ordinance, it was never enforced. It was not until the Code Napoléon was promulgated, that a will in the olographic form, without witnesses, was valid throughout France.

François Xavier Martin, Chief Justice of Louisiana, died in 1846,.leaving an olographic will executed in 1844, when he had become blind, and remained so till his death. Its validity was questioned for want of capacity on the part of a blind man to make an olographic will, and because he could not read what he had written, and he could not write without the assistance of others to guide his hand. After the most elaborate discussion and a careful scrutiny of the conflicting views of foreign jurists, the Supreme Court maintained the will, partly because the testator himself, having evinced his opinion by writing the will, had great weight as an authority. (State *vs.* Martin, 2 A. 680.)

The code allows a soldier in the field to execute a will in presence of a commissioned officer and two witnesses. It must be signed by the testator, and remains operative for six months after the emergency has ceased.

The nuncupative will, if executed before a notary, must be attested by three witnesses, otherwise by five.

It is called nuncupative because it is read aloud by or to the testator in presence of the witnesses. A will not so read is called mystic, and being signed must be presented by the testator to a notary, and sealed up in presence of seven witnesses. Persons under sixteen years of age, and women, cannot be witnesses. At sixteen, a man or woman, married or unmarried, has capacity to make a will.

The exclusion of women as witnesses is attributed to the influence of the *sacra gentilica* of ancient Rome, when wills were executed subject to the confirmation of public assemblies, to which women were not admitted—"*ab omnibus officiis civilibus vel publicis remotæ.*"

A testament clothed with the formalities prescribed by the law of the place of its execution will be enforced in Louisiana, both as to real and personal property, although it would be void as to form, if executed in the state. This doctrine applies even to citizens of the state who make wills abroad. A will becomes void on the birth of a child posterior to its execution; so that a married man with a fruitful wife might have to make a dozen wills in as many years; and even then the birth of a posthumous child would frustrate his testamentary aspirations, so that one may die apparently testate, yet become intestate by an event occurring after death.

In point of law, however, a child conceived, if subsequently born alive, is reputed to have been born at the date of conception, and therefore the posthumous child in the case supposed is reputed born before its parents death. Although husband and wife during marriage may make donations to one another, such donations are revocable at the pleasure of the donor; but they cannot by the same will or act of donation make to each other mutual or reciprocal donations or bequests; nor can two or more persons make a will in one and the same act. These prohibitions are founded on the absolute revocability of all wills and of donations *inter vivos* between married persons. Reciprocal wills, or donations between married persons in the same act, carry the implication of mutual understanding or agreement, which is antagonistic to absolute freedom of revocation.

Marriage alone, either of man or woman, will not revoke a will; nor can the testator, by any provision in the will, prevent its revocation by the subsequent birth of a child.

No gift *mortis causa* can be made otherwise than by testament. Every other form is abrogated. (C. C. 1,750.)

A donation *inter vivos* can comprehend only the present property of the donor. If it comprehends future acquired property, it is null as to that.

A donation *inter vivos* is an act by which the donor divests himself at present and irrevocably of the thing given. He may stipulate for the return of the thing to him in case he survive the donee and his descendants; and he may revoke the donation for ingratitude on the part of the donee—that is to say, if the donee attempt to take his life, or is guilty of cruel treatment or of crimes towards him, or if he has refused him food in distress. (C. C. 1,560.)

The donor cannot reserve to himself the usufruct of the thing given; but on the other hand he cannot divest himself of all his property; and therefore, unless he reserve enough for his subsistence, the entire donation is void. (C. C. 1,407.) The law will not allow him to strip himself *omnium bonorum.*

There is some modification of the rules governing donations *inter vivos* in general, when those donations are made in favor of marriage to the husband or wife by fathers, mothers, or other ascendants, and even by strangers. In such donations, the donor may give the whole or a part of the property he shall have on the day of his decease for the benefit of the parties to the marriage, and in case the donor survive the donee, for the benefit of the children or other descendants to proceed from that marriage. Such donations may embrace property acquired and to be acquired; and they are irrevocable only in the sense that the donor can no longer dispose of the objects comprised in the donation by gratuitous title, but he retains the full liberty of selling and mortgaging, unless he has formerly renounced that right.

It is perceived that this class of donations is peculiar. In a donation *inter vivos* proper, the donor divests himself at present and irrevocably of the thing given, and it cannot embrace future acquired property; whereas, the donation in favor of marriage may embrace present and future property, and is revocable to the extent to which the power to alienate is reserved to the donor, and inures to the benefit of children not *in esse* at the date of the donation; and in case the donee dies without children or descendants, the donation is of no effect.

It is a hybrid donation, called by the French, *l'institution contractuelle,* or the institution of heir by contract.

It confers an eventual right to the succession of the donor, who cannot give away or bequeath his property to a third person, though he may sell it, unless he has expressly debarred himself of that right; but while the donor is alive, the donee has no right in the property, and in this respect his interest resembles that of a presumptive heir. His right is a right to the faculty of becoming heir, if he is alive at the death of the donor.

There is also a limitation on the power of married persons to make donations to one another, where the donor has children by a previous marriage. In such case the donor can give to the new spouse only one-third of his estate. (Act of 1882.)

A second marriage, where there are children of the preceding marriage, destroys the power of the party contracting it to dispose of the property given or bequeathed to him or her by the deceased spouse. Such property on the second marriage is, by operation of law, vested in the children of the first marriage, and the spouse who marries again has only the usufruct of it. (C. C. Arts. 1,752, 1,753.) These provisions are of Roman origin. The Justinian Code and the 98th Novel first limited the power of donation in case of second marriage. This power was still further contracted by Theodosius the Great, and Theodosius the Second, and Valentian the Third.

The object of a marriage contract in Louisiana is to designate the property constituting the dowry, which the wife brings to the husband to support the expenses of the marriage. Whatever property is declared in the marriage contract to belong to the wife, or to be given to her on account of the marriage, by other persons than the husband, is a part of the dowry. Such property is called dotal. It can only be settled by a marriage contract, evidenced by authentic act executed before marriage. In no other form is it valid, nor can it be executed after marriage, nor can the dowry be increased during the marriage.

The income of dotal property belongs to the husband, to help him to support the charges of the marriage. He alone has the administration of it.

As a general rule, dotal immovables are inalienable during the marriage. The marriage contract may allow them to be sold, but in such case their value must be invested in other immovables, which become dotal. The purchaser, however, is not bound to see to the application of the purchase money.

Under special circumstances the wife, with the assent of her husband, and on the authorization of the judge of her domicile, given after an examination apart from her husband, may mortgage dotal property to raise money for her own use and benefit.

The wife may also, with the consent of her husband, provide for the establishment of their children by gifts of dotal property. The court, however, may order the sale of dotal immovables at public auction, when necessary for the maintenance of the family or for the payment of ante-nuptial debts of the wife, or for the purpose of making heavy repairs, indispensably necessary for the preservation of the immovables settled as dowry.

The obligations of the husband in respect to dotal property are those of an usufructuary. He becomes owner of the movables valued in the marriage contract, unless the contrary is declared. He is obliged to restore the movables or their value on the dissolution of the marriage, and the wife has a legal mortgage on the immovables, and a privilege on the movables of her husband, for the restitution of her dowry. A legal mortgage is a right of mortgage given by law without any stipulation of the parties. It is also called tacit, because it is established by law, without the aid of any agreement. The wife has also a legal mortgage for the restitution of her paraphernal property; so has a

minor on the immovables of his tutor, and persons inter-
dicted on the immovables of their curators.   Formerly this
legal or tacit mortgage affected all the immovables of the
debtor in the state, without registration ; now, provision is
made for recording the evidence of claims to which the law
attaches a right of mortgage, and thereby the inconveniences
of the tacit mortgage system have been reached.

All property belonging to the wife at the time of marriage, or inherited by, or given to her after the marriage, is
her separate property, and is called paraphernal or extra dotal.
Her husband has no interest whatever in it, nor has she any
interest in the property owned by him at the time of the marriage, or subsequently inherited or acquired by donation.

The wife is entitled to the administration of her paraphernal
property, and to the enjoyment of the revenues and fruits
thereof; but she cannot alienate or mortgage it without the
consent of her husband.   If he administers it against her will,
he is accountable for all the fruits and revenues received by
him, and she can restrain him from further interference ; but
he is not responsible for the ante-nuptial debts of the wife.

Every marriage contracted in the state superinduces of
right the conjugal partnership or community of acquets
and gains, if there be no stipulations to the contrary in the
marriage contract.

All property which is not dotal or paraphernal belongs to
the community; that is to say:

First. The fruits of the property of which the husband
has the administration and enjoyment of right or in fact.
This includes the revenues of the husband's separate property, and of the wife's paraphernal property, if she allows
him to administer it.

Second. The produce of the labor or industry of the husband or wife.   This includes every species of profit, the
result of toil or talent.

Third. All property purchased by husband or wife, unless it be as an investment of paraphernal funds.

Fourth. All donations *inter vivos* or *mortis causa* made jointly to both husband and wife.

Fifth. The value of the improvements put on the separate property of either spouse, and paid for with funds of the community. During the marriage, the title to the community property is vested in the husband. He is the head and master of the community. He disposes of its revenues and alienates its property without the consent of his wife; but he cannot give it away, except for the establishment of the children of the marriage; he may, however, make particular gifts of movable effects.

If the husband should sell or otherwise dispose of the community property for the purpose of defrauding his wife, she is entitled to restitution against him or his heirs on the dissolution of the community. The title of the wife to any special or proprietary interest does not vest until the dissolution of the community; until then she has only a contingent and eventual right in one-half of such of the acquets and gains as may be found in the possession of the community at its termination. Even then her right is contingent on her acceptance of the community, which involves responsibility for one-half the debts, unless she accepts with benefit of inventory, which she may now do. If she does not accept, she is as much a stranger to the property as if no community had ever existed.

The community is dissolved by—1, death of either spouse; 2, a judgment annulling a putative marriage; 3, a judgment giving to the heirs of an absentee provisional possession of his estate; 4, a separation of property, which is effected by a judgment in an action instituted by the wife for that purpose, or flows as a necessary consequence from a judgment of separation *a mensa et thoro,* or of divorce *a vinculo matrimonii.*

It is only the wife who can institute an action for separation of property, and thereby dissolve the community; this right is given to her when the disorder of her husband's affairs induces her to believe that his estate is insufficient to meet her claims against him, or when he neglects to reinvest the dotal effects according to law, or when he is insolvent, and she desires to preserve for herself and her children the fruits of her industry. Such fruits would otherwise fall into the community, and be subject to seizure for the husband's debts.

The policy of the law favors the community, and therefore a separation of property sought for can only be decreed by a court of justice, after hearing all the parties, and on proof of the requisite facts. The community of Louisiana is of Spanish origin and is much more simple than that of France.

Time forbids a discussion of the theory of obligations. For that reason I confine myself to a meagre statement of a few elementary principles.

A civil obligation is defined in the code to be a legal tie, which gives the party with whom it is contracted the right of enforcing its performance by law.

The sources of obligation are five: 1, contract; 2, quasi-contract: 3, offense; 4, quasi-offense; 5, the law.

It is said by Maine that the Greek word *nomos* (law) does not occur in Homer.

The terms "contract" and "obligation of contract" are not to be found in the English Bible or in the writings of Lord Coke; Shakespeare makes Hamlet say, in alluding to the marriage of his mother,

> "O such a deed
> As from the body of contraction plucks the very soul!"

but the expression refers to the exceptional contract of marriage between royal persons. "Agreement" and "covenant" were the law terms used by common law writers until within the last two hundred year, and Powell, in the present century, was the first common law author of a treatise on contracts.

Yet neither the term "agreement" nor "covenant" conveys the full and complete idea of a contract as understood by the civilians; for a contract gives rise to civil obligations, and is therefore classed as one of the sources of obligations; and the dominant idea of a civil obligation is the "*juris vinculum quo necessitate astringimur alicujus rei solvendæ, secundum nostræ civitatis jura.*"

The absence of this *juris vinculum* from an "agreement" or "covenant," for any reason whatever, deprives it of the character of a contract, because it is not susceptible of execution by an appeal to the public force of the country through its judicial tribunals. It is for this reason that the public debt of a nation, the holders of which have no right of action, does not fall within the category of civil obligations. The public debt is, as Hamilton said, "A property subsisting in the faith of the government. Its essence is promise. Its definite value depends upon the reliance that the promise will be definitely fulfilled." The government represents the public probity, and its high mission and weighty responsibilities afford guarantees which satisfy creditors as well as society itself.

There are two elements necessary to constitute an obligation:

First. The *juris vinculum*, by which an obligor can be sued in a court of justice, and compelled by the public force to comply with his obligation.

Second. It must exist before one or more determinate persons on the one side, and one or more determinate persons on the other side. It is essentially individual and relative, and must not be confounded with general duty to society.

It is true there is a general obligation not to assail a man's person or property; but this is an obligation common to all persons, and is of a negative, not of a positive, character, and does not bind one determinate person to another determinate person. On the contrary, it is obligatory upon all persons towards one another. It is called social duty, and is only the respect due to real rights.

1. Quasi-contracts are the lawful and purely voluntary acts of a man, from which there results any obligation whatever to a third person, and sometimes a reciprocal obligation between the parties.

This class of obligation arises from *lawful acts*, and not from agreements. Illustrations of quasi-contracts are the obligations arising when a man, of his own accord, undertakes the management of the affairs of another, under circumstances from which no agency can be inferred. His obligations as *negotiorum gestor* are those of a quasi-contract; the obligation to restore money paid or received in error is a quasi-contract; all the equitable doctrine that no man shall enrich himself at the expense of another comes under this head. An heir benefited by a third person's payment of his ancestor's debts, although payment is not made at the request of the heir or ancestor, is bound by a quasi-contract to reimburse the amount so paid. Hence it is perceived the quasi-contract is not the implied contract of the common law, which presupposes the request of the party who receives the benefit. The obligation of the quasi-contract results from benefit actually received from a lawful act done without request.

2. An offense is an illegal act done, with intent to injure.

3. A quasi-offense is an unlawful act done unintentionally, the result of negligence or imprudence.

The injury resulting from an offense or quasi-offense gives rise to an obligation to repair it. The code sententiously declares that "every act whatever of man that causes damage to another obliges him by whose fault it happened to repair it."

4. Illustrations of obligations resulting from the operation of the law are the obligation to pay taxes, and in Louisiana the obligation to allow your neighbor, in cities, to rest nine inches of his wall on your land.

It is considered by civilians, that the classification I have mentioned embraces every conceivable condition of fact giving rise to civil obligations.

I pretermit also the doctrine of privileges, a privilege being a right which the nature of the debt gives to the creditor, and which entitles him to be preferred to other creditors, even those who have mortgages. It is conferred by law, and cannot be created by contract.

The privilege is either general—that is to say, it affects all the property of the debtor, or all his movables—or is special—that is to say, is applicable to a particular object, as in the case of the vendor, who has a privilege on the thing sold for the unpaid price.

While a privilege may affect movables, a mortgage cannot; for movables are not susceptible of mortgage.

The general privileges on all the property of the debtor are funeral charges, judicial charges, expenses of the last illness, wages of servants, and salaries of clerks for the year past, and so much as is due for the current year.

The dotal, but not the paraphernal, rights of the wife are secured by a general privilege on all the movables of the husband.

A debt for supplies of provisions to the debtor or his family during the last six months by retail dealers is entitled to a similar privilege. In addition to the privilege given to the vendor for the unpaid price of the object sold, the law implies in the contract of sale, and in every commutative or synallagmatic contract, a resolutory condition, which gives either party the right to sue for a revocation of the contract in case the other fails to comply with his engagements. Both the privilege of the vendor and the resolutory condition were unknown to the Roman law ; for after delivery, that law abandoned the vendor selling on credit to the good faith of the purchaser, and refused a resolution of the sale for non-payment of the price, unless the *pactum commissorium* had been expressly stipulated.

The privilege of the vendor and the resolutory condition are the conception of the modern civilians, who say that both rights are visceral to the contract of sale (*adhærent visceribus rei*), and therefore exist, unless renounced in terms not to be mistaken.

In conclusion, I must barely allude to the third mode of acquisition—the operation of the law.

Under this head is embraced acquisition by accession, occupancy, prescription, and the perception of fruits by a *bona fide* possessor. The Code of 1808 admitted seven modes of acquisition. The existing code has included in one class, "the operation of the law," all other modes than succession and the effect of obligations.

The right of accession is the right of the owner of a thing to all that it produces, or becomes united to or incorporated with it, either naturally or artificially ; as, for instance, fruits, accretions, or the union of two things by adjunction, as a picture to a frame ; or by specification, as where a block of marble has been converted into an Apollo by a sculptor ; or by commixtion or confusion, as in the case of the mixture of wines belonging to different proprietors.

Acquisition by occupancy requires no comment, nor does that by prescription. I should remark, however, that there are two kinds of prescription : one termed liberative, which discharges a person from debt ; the other called acquisitive, because thereby property is acquired. The liberative prescription differs from the common law Statute of Limitations in this, that it is extinctive in its character, and therefore is defined in the code as one of the modes of extinguishing obligations. Hence it is not the debtor alone who can plead prescription, as is the case at common law, but creditors, and all other persons who may have an interest in acquiring an estate or extinguishing an obligation may plead it, even though the debtor should refuse to make the plea or renounce it.

The perception of fruits by a *bona fide* possessor is a mode of acquisition, because, although he is not owner, yet, believing himself to be so, the law gives him the fruits of the thing in his possession, while he is ignorant of the defects of his title.

Milton Keynes UK
Ingram Content Group UK Ltd.
UKHW040931180224
437992UK00003B/168

9 783385 332270